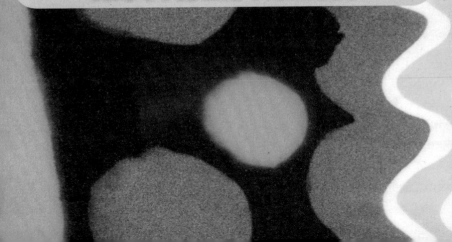

The Present Moment

ALSO BY LOUISE HAY

BOOKS/KITS

Colors & Numbers

Empowering Women

Everyday Positive Thinking

Experience Your Good Now!
(book-with-CD)

*A Garden of Thoughts: My
Affirmation Journal*

Gratitude: A Way of Life
(Louise & Friends)

Heal Your Body

Heal Your Body A–Z Heart Thoughts
(also available in a gift edition)

I Can Do It® (book-with-CD)

Inner Wisdom

Letters to Louise

Life! Reflections on Your Journey

Love Your Body

*Love Yourself, Heal Your Life
Workbook*

Meditations to Heal Your Life
(also available in a gift edition)

Modern-Day Miracles

The Power Is Within You

Power Thoughts

The Times of Our Lives
(Louise & Friends)

You Can Create an Exceptional Life
(with Cheryl Richardson)

You Can Heal Your Life
(also available in a gift edition)

*You Can Heal Your Life
Affirmation Kit*

*You Can Heal Your Life
Companion Book*

FOR CHILDREN

The Adventures of Lulu

I Think, I Am! (with Kristina Tracy)

Lulu and the Ant: A Message of Love

*Lulu and the Dark:
Conquering Fears*

*Lulu and Willy the Duck:
Learning Mirror Work*

CD PROGRAMS

Anger Releasing

Cancer

Change and Transition

Dissolving Barriers

Embracing Change

The Empowering Women Gift Collection

Feeling Fine Affirmations

Forgiveness/Loving the Inner Child

How to Love Yourself

Meditations for Personal Healing

Meditations to Heal Your Life (audio book)

Morning and Evening Meditations

101 Power Thoughts

Overcoming Fears

The Power Is Within You (audio book)

The Power of Your Spoken Word

Receiving Prosperity

Self-Esteem Affirmations (subliminal)

Self-Healing

Stress-Free (subliminal)

Totality of Possibilities

What I Believe and Deep Relaxation

You Can Heal Your Life (audio book)

You Can Heal Your Life Study Course

Your Thoughts Create Your Life

DVDs

Dissolving Barriers

Receiving Prosperity

You Can Heal Your Life Study Course

You Can Heal Your Life, The Movie (also available in an expanded edition)

CARD DECKS

Healthy Body Cards

I Can Do It® Cards

I Can Do It® Cards . . . for Creativity, Forgiveness, Health, Job Success, Wealth, Romance

Power Thought Cards

Power Thoughts for Teens

Power Thought Sticky Cards

Wisdom Cards

CALENDAR

I Can Do It® *Calendar* (for each individual year)

and

THE LOUISE HAY BOOK COLLECTION

(comprising the gift versions of *Meditations to Heal Your Life, You Can Heal Your Life,* and *You Can Heal Your Life Companion Book*)

All of the above are available at your local
bookstore, or may be ordered by visiting:

Hay House USA: **www.hayhouse.com**®
Hay House Australia: **www.hayhouse.com.au**
Hay House UK: **www.hayhouse.co.uk**
Hay House South Africa: **www.hayhouse.co.za**
Hay House India: **www.hayhouse.co.in**

Louise's website: **www.LouiseHay.com**®

The Present Moment

365 Daily Affirmations

Louise Hay

HAY HOUSE, INC.
Carlsbad, California • New York City
London • Sydney • Johannesburg
Vancouver • Hong Kong • New Delhi

Copyright © 2007 by Louise Hay

Published and distributed in the United States by: Hay House, Inc.: www.hayhouse.com • **Published and distributed in Australia by:** Hay House Australia Pty. Ltd.: www.hayhouse.com.au • **Published and distributed in the United Kingdom by:** Hay House UK, Ltd.: www.hayhouse.co.uk • **Published and distributed in the Republic of South Africa by:** Hay House SA (Pty), Ltd.: www.hayhouse.co.za • **Distributed in Canada by:** Raincoast Books: www.raincoast.com • **Published in India by:** Hay House Publishers India: www.hayhouse.co.in

Editorial supervision: Jill Kramer   **Design:** Nick Welch   **Illustrations:** Digital Stock

The material in this book is adapted from the *I Can Do It® 2006 Calendar*, by Louise Hay.

Library of Congress Control Number: 2005939097

ISBN: 978-1-4019-1194-2

14 13 12 11 10 9 8 7 6 5
1st edition, August 2007

Introduction

This little book is filled with positive affirmations that will show you that your point of power is always in the present moment, and this is where you plant the mental seeds for creating new experiences. You're never stuck, for you can choose new thoughts and new ways of thinking. Your future can always be more positive, more loving, and more prosperous.

Think about how you'd like to live and what you'd like to accomplish. Each day I will help guide your thinking in positive ways to accomplish these goals. As you read this work, you'll find that you develop new mental habits that you can use for the rest of your life!

— **Louise Hay**

1

Life supports me and wants me to be fulfilled and happy.

This is a great day to create, imagine, produce, and visualize.

I see the world
through eyes
of love.

My job supports the unfoldment of my highest potential.

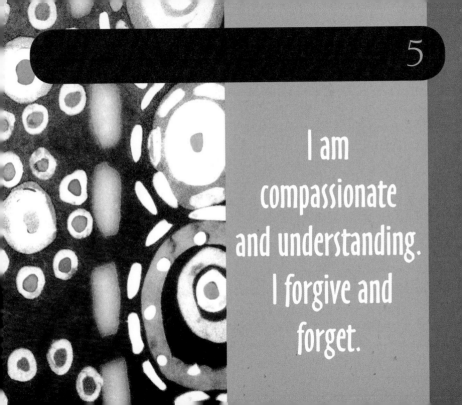

5

I am compassionate and understanding. I forgive and forget.

My body is always working toward optimal health. I am happy and healthy.

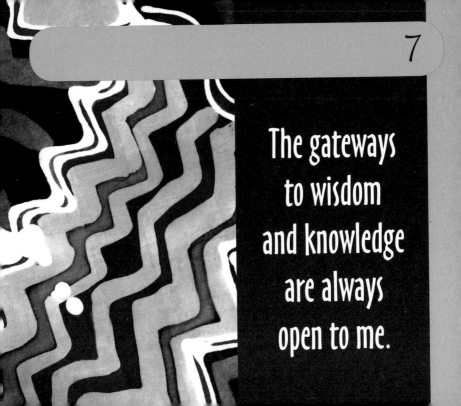

The gateways
to wisdom
and knowledge
are always
open to me.

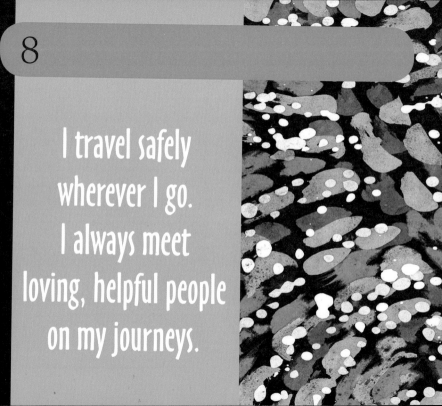

8

I travel safely
wherever I go.
I always meet
loving, helpful people
on my journeys.

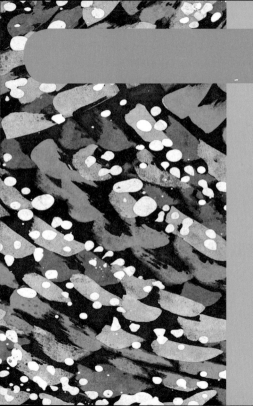

I eagerly look forward to the future.

10

I radiate success,
and I prosper
wherever I turn.

My grateful heart recharges my soul and revitalizes my body.

People respect me and are very appreciative of everything I do.

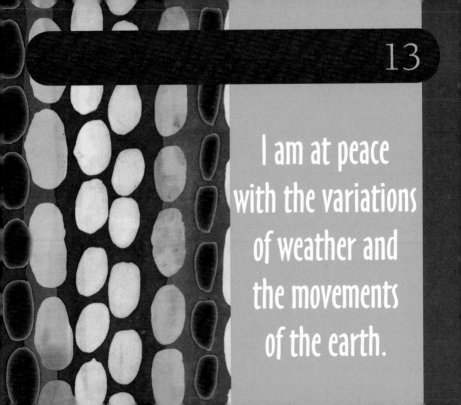

13

I am at peace
with the variations
of weather and
the movements
of the earth.

14

I accept every part of me, even the parts I am just learning to like.

My health
gets better
and better
all the time.

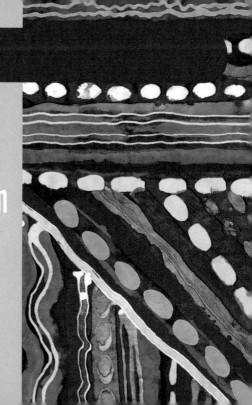

Equality and world peace begin with me. Today I express loving kindness to all.

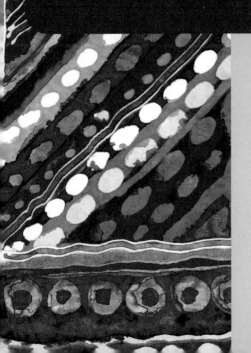

I handle
my life with
joy and ease.

My work gives
me great
pleasure.

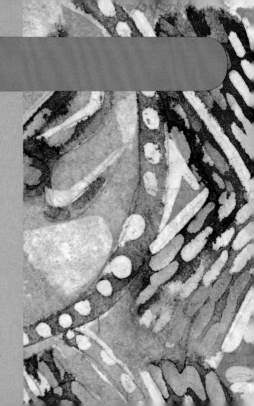

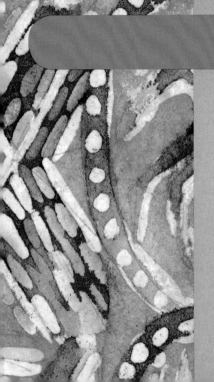

Abundance is drawn
to my every action.
I am a magnet for
Divine prosperity.

I am patient, tolerant, and diplomatic.

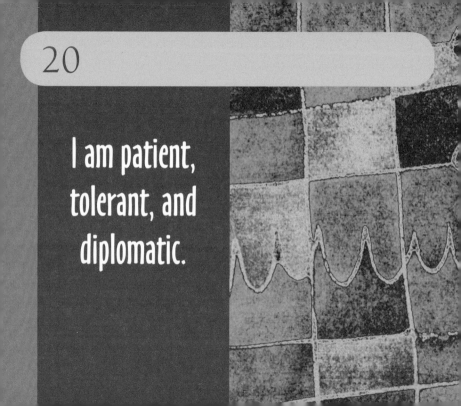

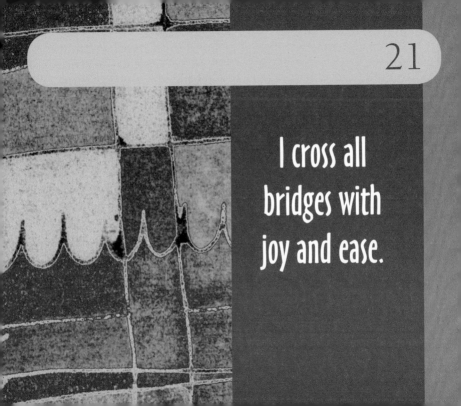

I cross all bridges with joy and ease.

I forgive all
past experiences.
I choose to live
in the joyous now.

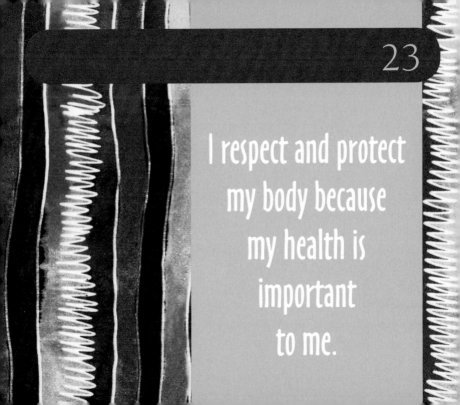

23

I respect and protect
my body because
my health is
important
to me.

I rise above all limitations. I am Divinely guided and inspired.

Life is really
very simple.
What we give out,
we get back.

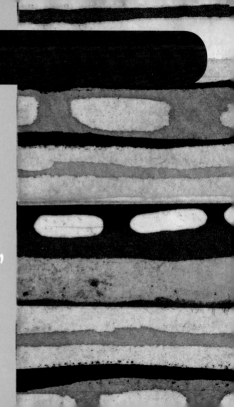

I am doing the
best I can with
the understanding,
knowledge, and
awareness I have.

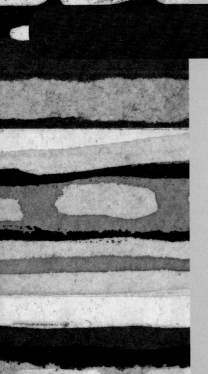

27

Today is a delightful day. Money comes to me in expected and unexpected ways.

Today I celebrate
all that I am
and all that
I will become.

The more
I love myself,
the younger
I look.

My job is fun, and my life is adventurous.

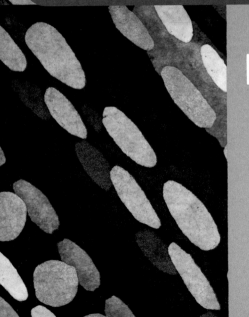

I listen with love
to my body's
messages.

I marvel at the beauty that surrounds me.

Wellness is the natural state of my body. I believe in perfect health.

Everyone I encounter today at work has my best interests at heart.

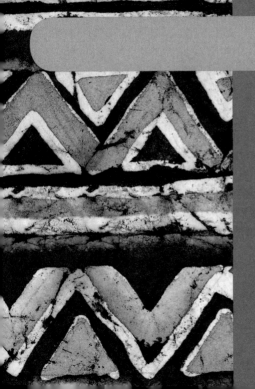

All this positive
self-talk is
paying off.
Life is good!

My partner and I are learning to accept each other totally. We release the need to blame each other, and know that we are both doing our best.

I only speak positively about those in my world. Negativity has no part in my life.

I feel glorious,
dynamic energy.
I am active
and alive.

Everything I touch is a success. I draw prosperity of every kind to me.

I rejoice in new growth. I leave all reservations behind me.

Love is the
miracle cure.
Loving myself
works miracles
in my life.

I lovingly and joyously accept my sexuality and its expression.

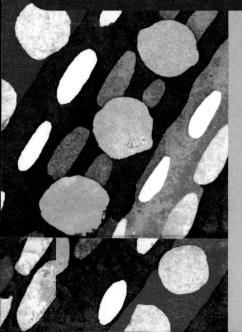

I give a portion
of my time to
helping others.
It is good for
my own health.

The past is over and cannot be changed. This is the only moment I can experience.

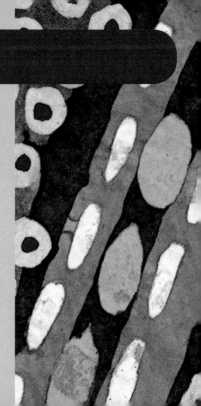

Love makes my world go 'round. My love goes out to touch others and returns to me multiplied.

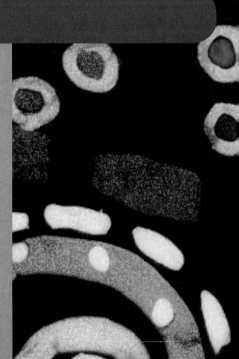

46

Changes can begin in this moment. I am willing to change.

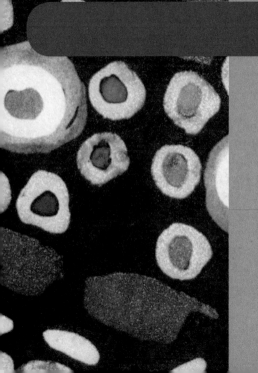

I am grateful
for life's
generosity
to me. I am
truly blessed.

I laugh at life
(and at myself),
and choose not to
be offended by
anyone or anything.

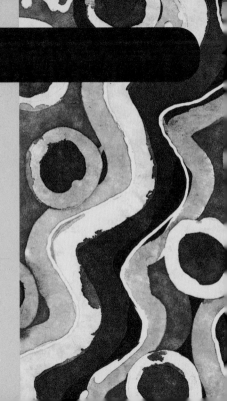

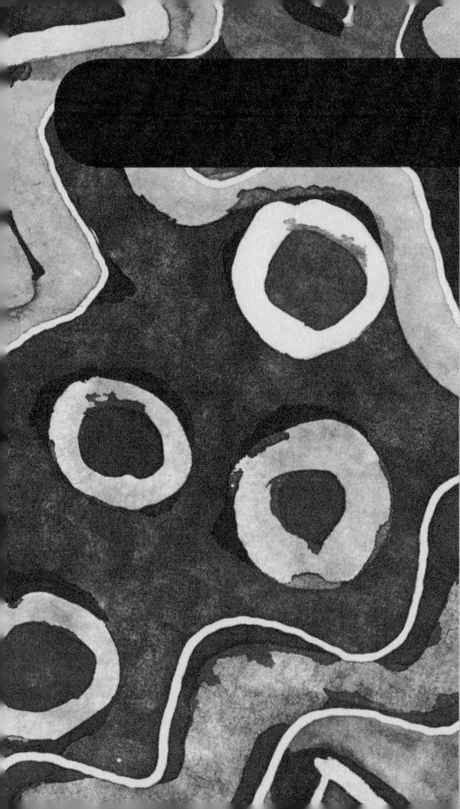

I am
at home
in my
body.

I now attract new friends who are exciting, loving, caring, accepting, funny, and generous.

I choose to make wise decisions that benefit every person, place, and thing in my world.

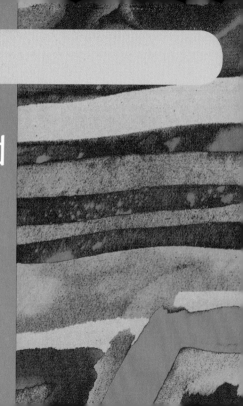

52

Everything I need
for my complete
healing comes
to me now.

I say *yes* to Life,
and Life abundantly
supplies me with
everything I need.

54

I am created to succeed, and I now give thanks for my success.

I see myself as
beautiful, lovable,
and appreciated.
I am proud to
be me.

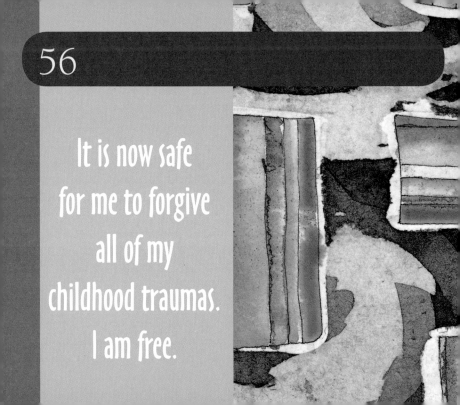

56

It is now safe
for me to forgive
all of my
childhood traumas.
I am free.

My home fulfills
all my needs
and desires.
I fill my home
with love.

I am responsible
for all of my
experiences.

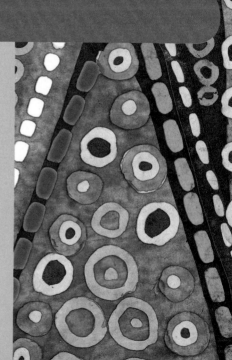

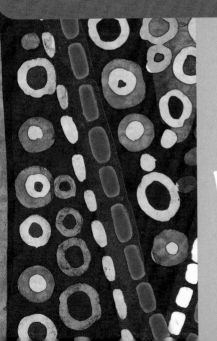

Whatever I am
guided to do
will be a success.

I allow my income
to constantly expand,
and I always live in
comfort and joy.

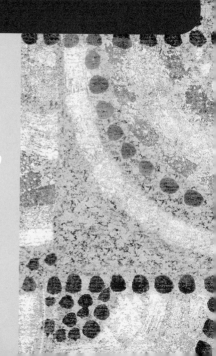

61

I create my own
experiences.
Life is fun!

Every bridge I cross brings me to a higher level of fulfillment.

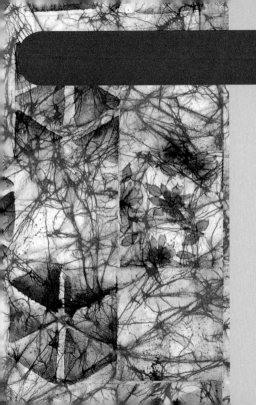

I feel great. People love being around me.

Peace begins with me.
The more peaceful
I am inside, the more
peace I have to share
with others.

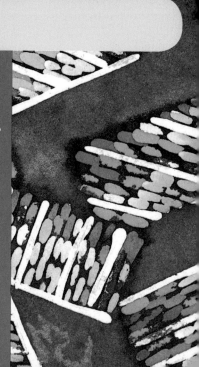

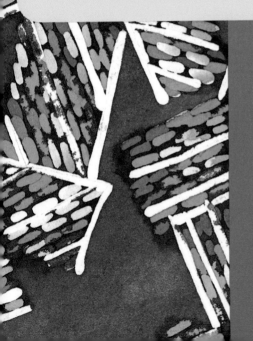

I delight in my
world, and my
world delights
in me.

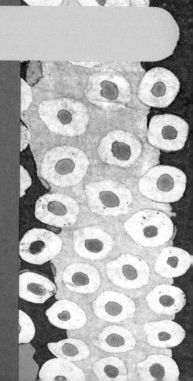

66

I bless my current job
with love and know
that it is only
a stepping-stone
on my pathway.

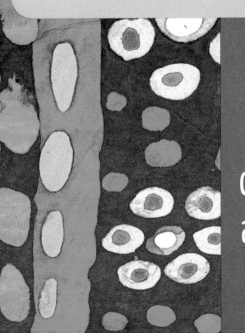

My mind is a tool that I can choose to use in any way I wish.

I am always
able to make the
correct decision.
I recognize my own
intuitive ability.

My good
comes from
everywhere and
everyone and
everything.

I am gentle, kind, and patient with myself. Those around me reflect this tender care.

All my needs and desires are met before I even ask. All is well in my world.

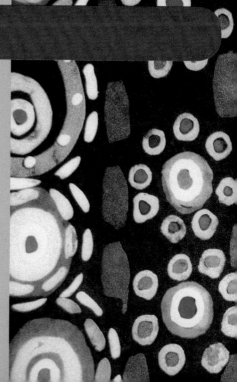

Today is the
future I created
yesterday.

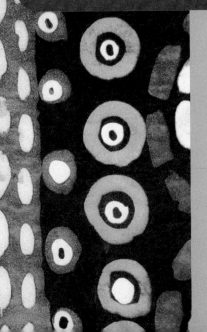

I listen with love to my body's messages. My body is the picture of total health.

Everyone changes,
and I allow change
in everyone.

I take full responsibility for every aspect of my life.

Green means "go," and I choose to go for all the good that life has in store for me.

I look within
to find my
treasures.

Other people respect me because I respect myself.

I look forward
with enthusiasm
to the adventures
of the day.

Spring is in
my heart.
I am dancing
on air!

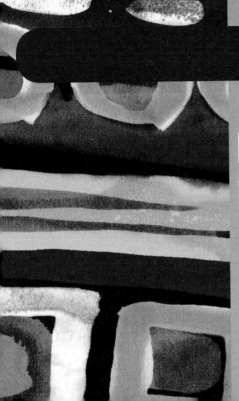

It is safe for me to be flexible enough to see others' viewpoints.

I speak up for myself with ease. I am intelligent and powerful.

I deserve the best,
and I accept it now.
All my needs and
desires are met
before I even ask.

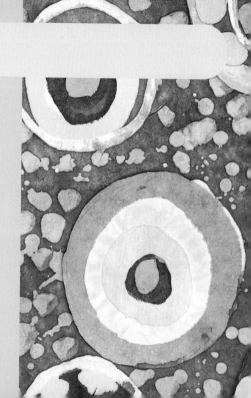

I now accept
and appreciate
the abundant
life the Universe
offers me.

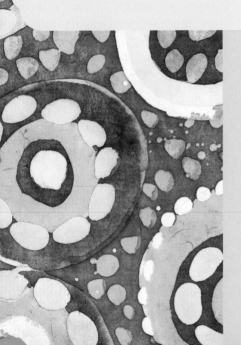

I breathe
freely and fully.
Breath is the
basis of life.

No person, place, or thing has any power over me, for I am the only thinker in my mind.

My body represents perfection. I am vibrantly healthy.

I always work
with and for
wonderful people.
I love my job.

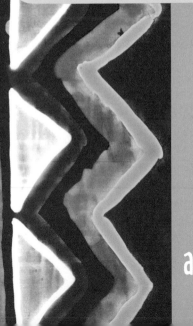

I read books that enrich my soul and give me food for thought. There is always more to learn.

I respect all
the members of
my family, and
they, in turn,
respect me.

I love life!
I look forward
to every
moment of it.

92

I have the
perfect living
space. It is safe,
and filled with
loving thoughts.

I eagerly
look
forward
to the
future.

I am as
successful as I
make up my
mind to be.

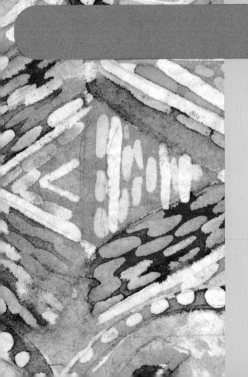

I recognize
my body as
a good friend.

I now release anger in positive ways. I love and appreciate myself.

I only speak words that are loving and constructive.

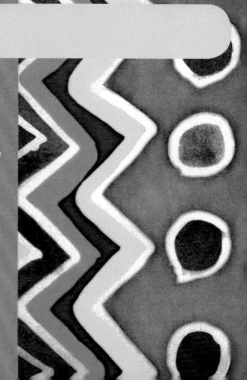

I take a deep breath and allow myself to relax. My whole body calms down.

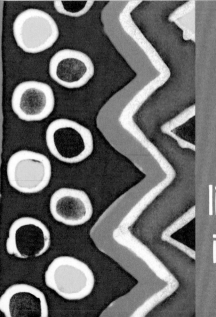

I grow beyond my family's limitations and live for myself. It is *my* turn now.

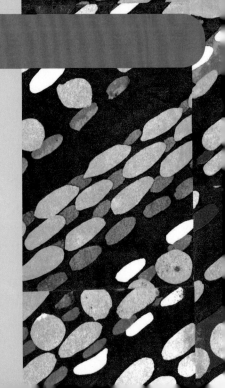

100

I rejoice in others' successes, knowing that there is plenty for us all.

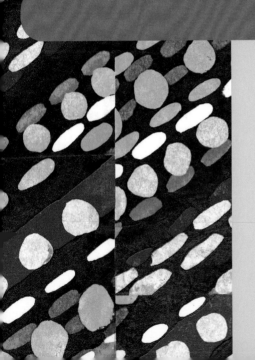

I am willing to release all patterns of criticism.

I become more lovable every day. I am seen by others as a loving, forgiving person.

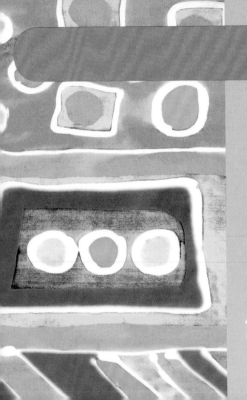

There is no need for me to struggle. I trust the Universe to take care of me.

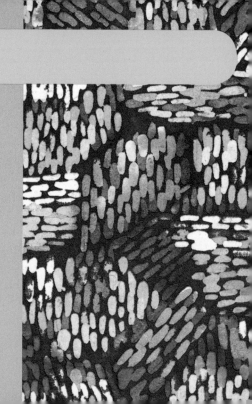

I have my
own set
of talents
and abilities.

Love
is all
there is!

The past has no power over me. I am renewed, refreshed, and reborn into a delicious new world.

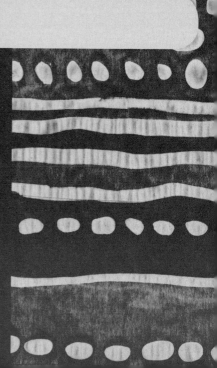

My inner quest is rewarding and provides me with many answers.

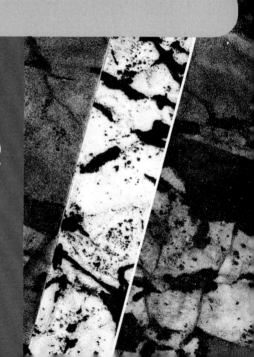

I am always
the perfect age
for where I am
in my life.

I work for
enjoyment and
satisfaction—
not just to earn
a living.

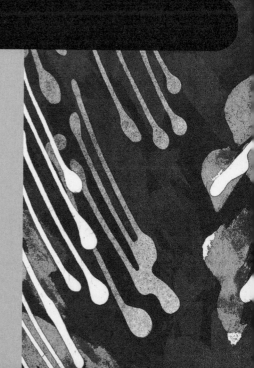

I rejoice in my body. I am glowing health personified.

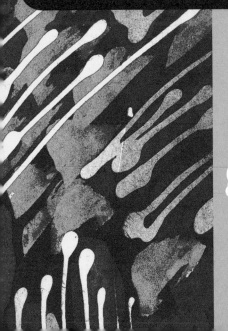

I go to sleep
at night feeling
great contentment.
I am at peace.

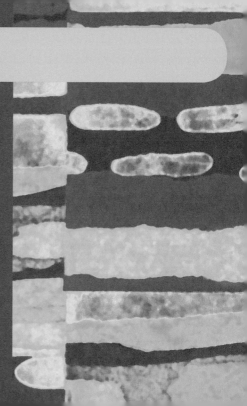

I keep my thoughts centered on what I wish to experience.

I release and let go. I gladly give away all that I no longer need.

I am joyous today.
Humor contributes
to my total
well-being.

I am totally
adequate for
all situations.

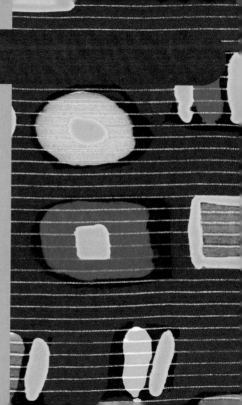

I lovingly accept
my decisions,
knowing that
I am free to
change them.

The love
from my heart
flows joyously
through my body.

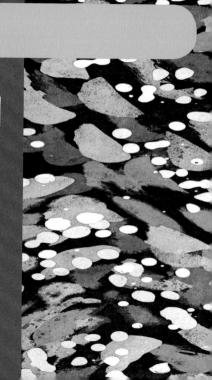

118

I open my home and welcome guests with music and love. My friends are like a loving family to me.

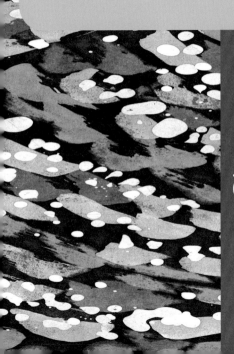

As I love and approve of myself and others, my life gets better and better.

I learn my
lessons in life
easily and
effortlessly.

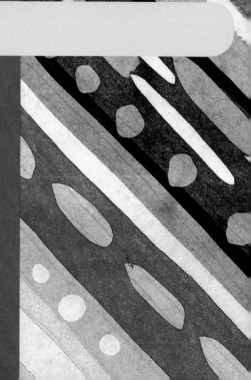

Forgiving makes
me feel free
and light.
I forgive everyone,
including myself.

I give love to all the animals that come into my life. They are gifts from the Universe.

I allow myself
to be open
and receptive
to learning
new ideas.

Good now flows into my life from expected and unexpected channels.

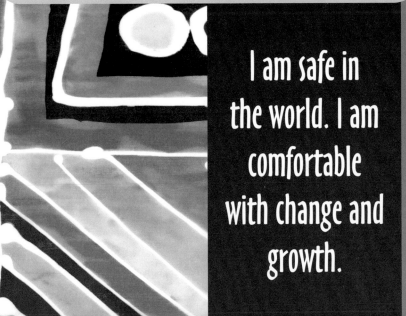

125

I am safe in the world. I am comfortable with change and growth.

Joyous new ideas
are circulating
freely within me.

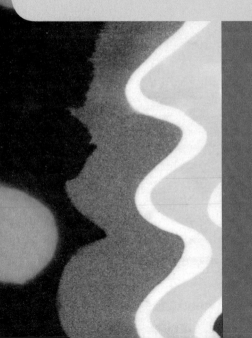

My day begins and ends with gratitude.

I am unlimited in my wealth. All areas of my life are abundant and fulfilling.

I effortlessly solve my problems by choosing positive thoughts.

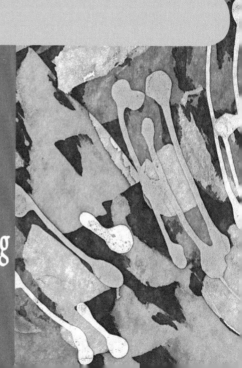

130

I am organized
and productive.
I am energetic,
and I enjoy getting
my life in order.

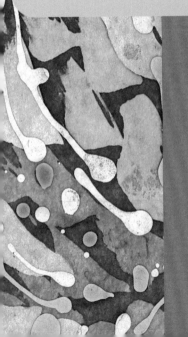

Knowing that friends
and lovers were once
strangers to me,
I welcome new
people into my life.

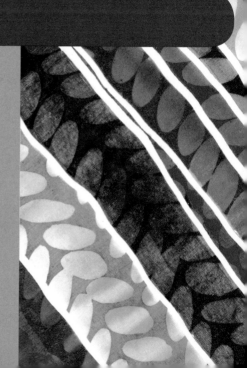

132

I am unlimited in my own ability to create the good in my life.

I view all experiences as opportunities for me to learn and grow.

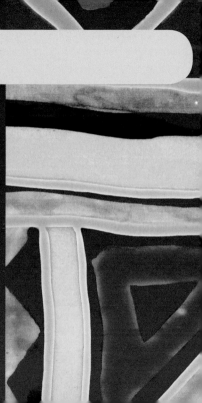

My mother has a special place in my heart. I think of my mother with love and gratitude.

I learn to
forgive and release.
Inner peace
is my goal.

No job is beneath or above me. If something needs doing, I do it.

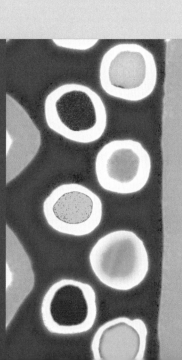

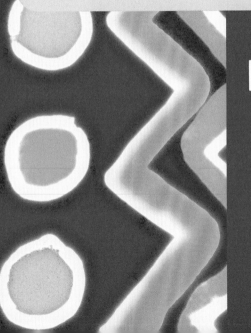

It is always easy
for me to adapt
and change.
I am flexible
and flowing.

138

I constantly
have new
insights.
My future is
glorious.

I am thankful
for all the
days I have
yet to live.
Life is so good.

I am at peace
with my sexuality.
I embrace myself
with love and
compassion.

I recognize my body as a wondrous machine, and I feel privileged to live in it.

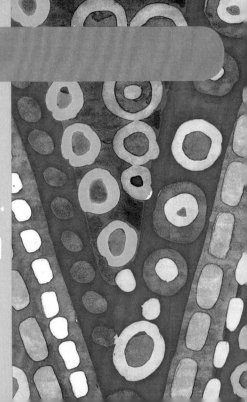

I am pleased
with all that I do.
I am good enough
just as I am.

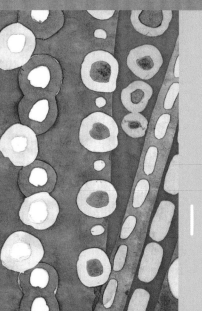

Freedom and
change are
in the air.
I discard old ideas.

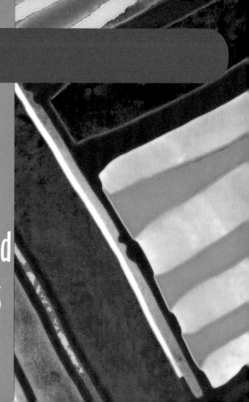

144

I feed my body
nourishing foods
and beverages, and
I exercise in ways
that are fun.

I am deeply
fulfilled by all
that I do.

The Ocean of Life is lavish with its abundance. Golden opportunities are everywhere.

With my loving attitude, I help to create a world where it is safe for us to love each other.

148

My heart is open.
I am willing
to release all
resistance.

Today I choose to reflect on all the wonderful things in my life.

150

I am the creative
power in my world.
I express myself
creatively as much
as possible.

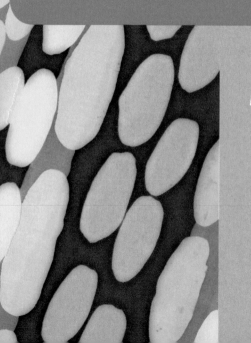

All that I seek
is already
within me.

152

I break new
ground and
begin exciting
and inspirational
ventures.

I am a decisive
and productive person.
I follow through with
tasks that I start and
make no excuses.

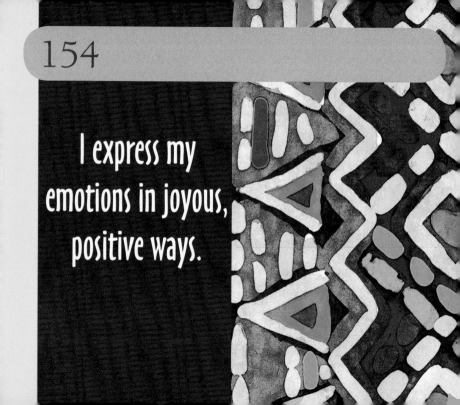

I express my emotions in joyous, positive ways.

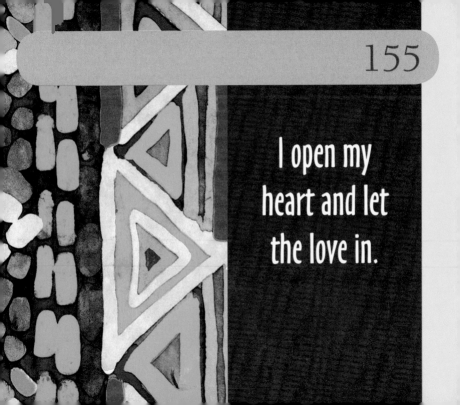

I open my heart and let the love in.

I feel the excitement and thrill of being alive today.

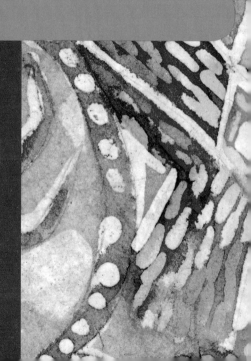

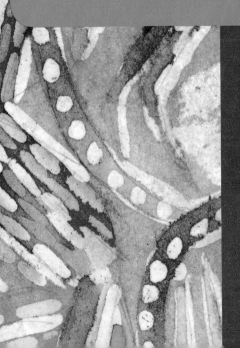

Within myself
I see a loving,
beautiful being.
It is safe for me
to look within.

It is my
birthright
to live fully
and freely.

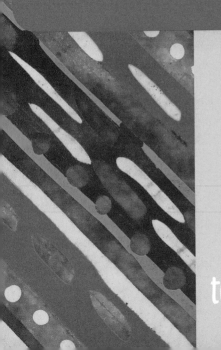

I am capable
and organized.
My efficiency is
more than ample
to get any job done.

My body wants to be active and healthy. Exercise is fun for me.

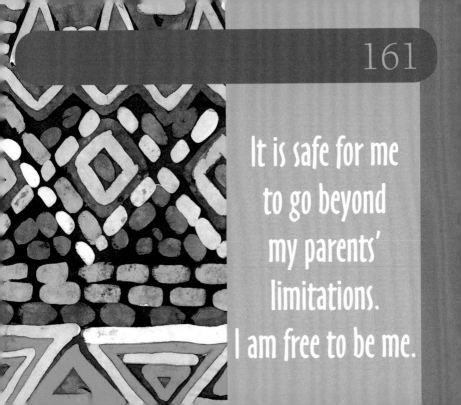

It is safe for me
to go beyond
my parents'
limitations.
I am free to be me.

I see the best in everyone and help them bring out their most joyous qualities.

I am an open channel for creative ideas.

Whatever I need to know is revealed to me at exactly the right time.

I am in total harmony
with my environment:
the sun, the moon,
the wind, the rain,
and the earth.

166

I am always presented with new and wonderful opportunities. I flow with what is happening in the moment.

I release all
struggle now,
and I am
at peace.

I release any limitations based on old, negative thoughts. I joyfully look forward to the future.

My heart
is receptive
and open.

I am enthusiastic about life. I am filled with energy and optimism.

I open new doors
to life. I am
confident that
all that is good is
coming to me.

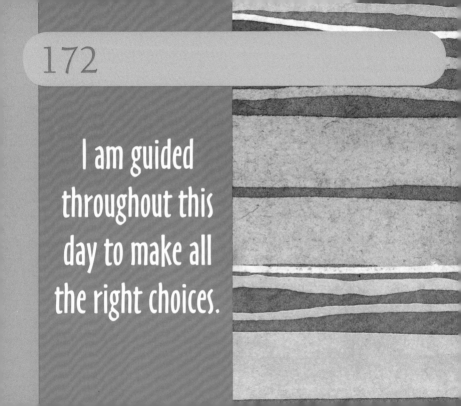

172

I am guided
throughout this
day to make all
the right choices.

People love to
be with me,
and I love to
be with them.

I am empowered
and confident.
I hold my head
up high.

I love
and cherish
my inner child.

I am in the perfect place at the perfect time. I am always safe.

Compliments are
gifts of prosperity.
I accept them
graciously.

Difficulties no longer burden me. I easily solve all problems.

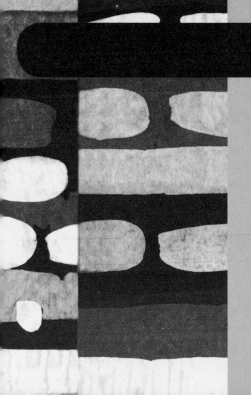

My thinking is peaceful, calm, and centered.

Divine peace and love surround me and dwell in me. I trust the process of life.

I take brisk walks in the sunshine to invigorate my body and soul.

182

I have the power
to create all that
I wish with my
thoughts.

My prosperous
affirmations create
my prosperous
world.

184

I am constantly moving forward in the direction of my goals.

I am free of the past. I declare my independence to be me!

Today I do a
mental housecleaning,
making room for new,
positive thoughts.

I am equally
blessed with love,
harmony, and joy.
My life is in
perfect balance.

I release the need to blame anyone, including myself.

I am special
and wonderful.
The more I love
myself, the less
stress I have.

I am one with the very Power that created me.

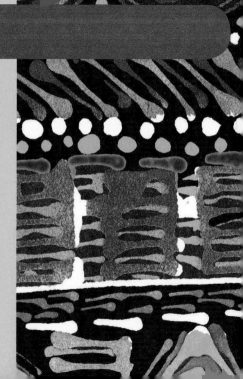

Every decision
I make is the
right one for me.

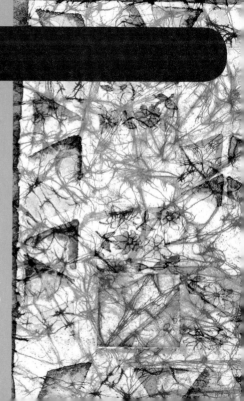

I ask for what
I want. I know
that whatever
I need will always
be there for me.

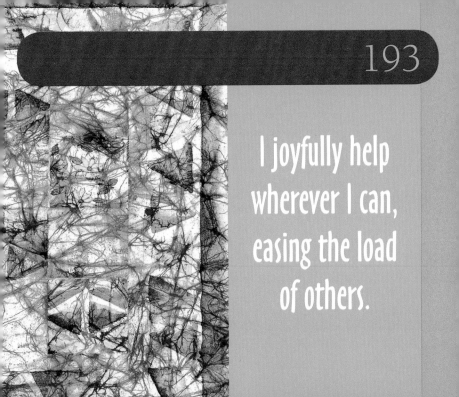

I joyfully help
wherever I can,
easing the load
of others.

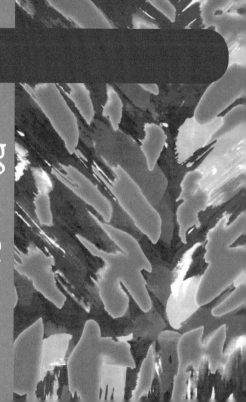

194

My understanding
is clear, and I am
willing to change
with the times.

I free myself
and everyone
in my life from
past hurts.

Every moment is
a new beginning.
My life is so sweet.

I love who I am
and what I do.

I accept perfect
health as my
natural state
of being.

All of my friends understand my needs. I have many friends who love me.

I recognize that awareness is the first step in healing or changing. I become more aware with each passing day.

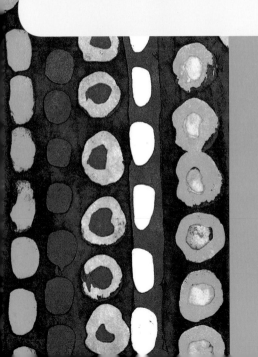

I am my own
best friend.
I love what
I see in me.

I try out new ideas. I am a leader today.

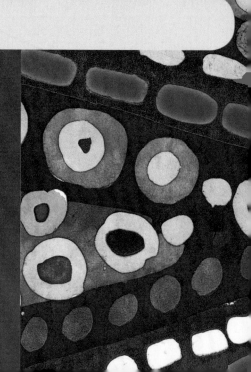

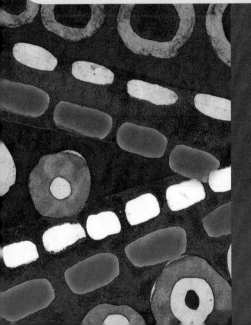

I am mentally and emotionally equipped to enjoy a loving, prosperous life.

My mind and body are in perfect balance. I am a harmonious being.

Today is my stepping-stone to new awareness and greater glory.

I radiate health,
happiness,
prosperity, and
peace of mind.

Every experience
I have benefits me.
I am in the process
of positive change.

208

Joy and beauty abound in my work space.

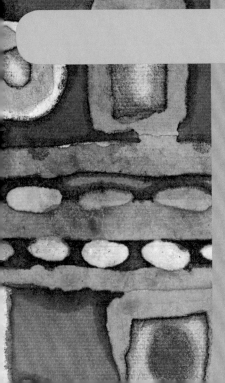

I am learning about love and respect at my job. I admire the people I work with.

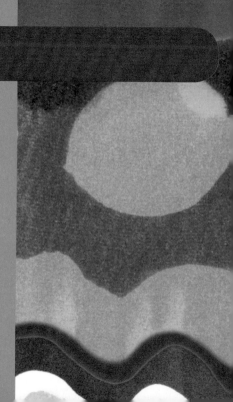

I feel tolerance, compassion, and love for everyone, myself included.

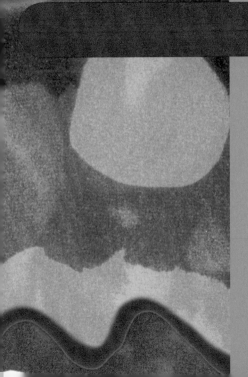

I accept
miraculous
occurrences in
my world.

It is healing to
show my emotions.
It is safe for me
to be vulnerable.

I can choose
to feel good
throughout
the day.

I am in charge.
I take my own
power back.

215

I give myself the green light to go ahead, and to joyously embrace the new.

216

I always feel appreciated at work. As I value life, life values me.

My body mirrors my state of mind. I am healthy, whole, and complete.

I stand in
truth and live
in joy.

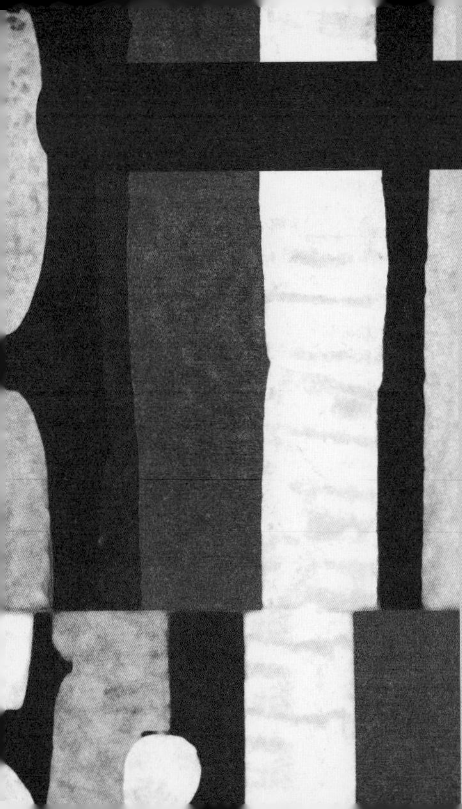

I bless and
prosper others;
and they,
in turn, bless
and prosper me.

220

I am in the right place at the right time, doing the right thing.

221

I feel reborn.
I am free of
the past, and I
joyously welcome
the new.

There is no "good" or "bad" weather. I can choose my individual reaction to it.

I now release all expectations, and I know that I am taken care of.

We are all family,
and the planet
is our home.

I am one with the power and wisdom of the Universe. I have all that I need.

When I listen
to my inner self,
I find the answers
I seek.

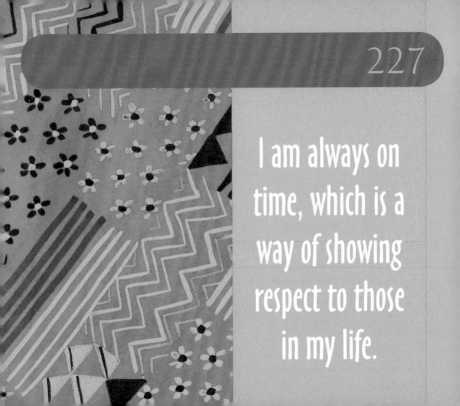

I am always on time, which is a way of showing respect to those in my life.

228

Love operates
in all of my
relationships, from
the most casual to
the most intimate.

I radiate warmth
and love.
I am beautiful,
and everyone
loves me.

My body takes me everywhere easily and effortlessly.

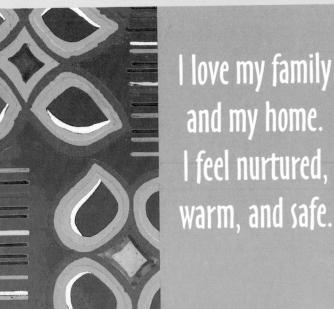

I love my family
and my home.
I feel nurtured,
warm, and safe.

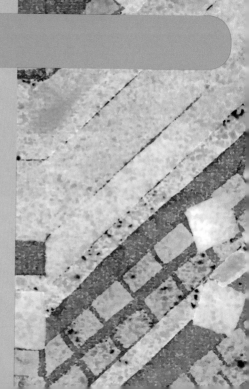

232

I now free myself from destructive fears and doubts.

I look forward
with joyous
anticipation to
the day.

I look and feel terrific.
Here I am, world—
open and receptive
to all good!

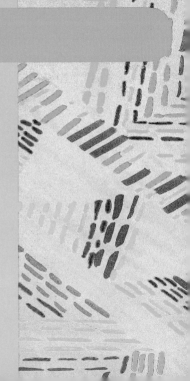

I see clearly.
I now create a
life I love
to look at.

I act with honor
and integrity in
all that I do.

I am the star
of my own movie,
and also the writer
and director. I create
wonderful roles for myself.

I trust my
Higher Self.
I listen with
love to my
inner voice.

I love
myself exactly
as I am.

240

All my relationships
are harmonious.
I see only harmony
around me at all
times.

I love my family members just as they are. I do not try to change anyone.

I now take care
of my body,
my mind, and
my emotions.
I feel good!

I experience
life as a
joyous dance.

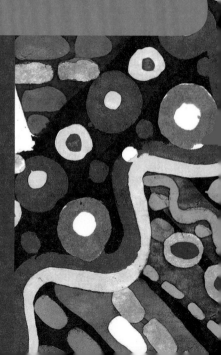

Everything I need
to know is brought
to me today in
delightful ways.

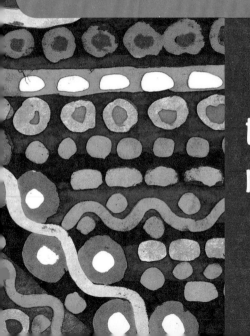

My joyful
thoughts create
my joyful world.

246

Every person, place, and thing on this planet is interconnected with love.

247

I am
at home
in the Universe.

There is ample time and opportunity for creative expression in whatever area I choose.

I am open and
receptive to all
the abundance that
surrounds me.

Opportunities are everywhere.
I have unlimited choices.

I truly believe that we
are here to bless and
prosper each other.
I reflect this belief in
my daily interactions.

I am proud that I can easily adapt to the ebb and flow of my life.

My body
is ideal
for me in
this lifetime.

I use my
power wisely.
I am strong,
and I am safe.

I release any feelings of competition or comparison. I simply do my best and enjoy being me.

I am willing to
learn to love
myself.

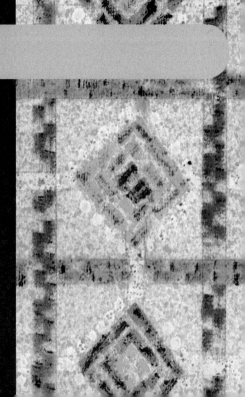

I speak positively
about others
and listen with
compassion.

My life continues to get better and better. I now move into my greater good.

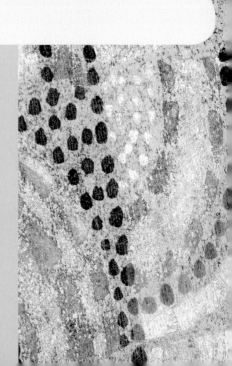

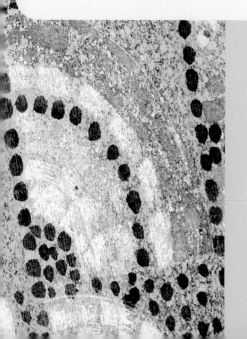

I breathe life
into my vision,
and I create the
world I desire.

260

I rejoice in what
I have, and I meet
all challenges
with open arms.

I am open
and receptive
to new avenues
of income.

Today is a
wonderful day.
I choose to
make it so.

I know that the point of power is always in the present moment.

I see myself as a magnificent being who is wise and beautiful. I love what I see in me.

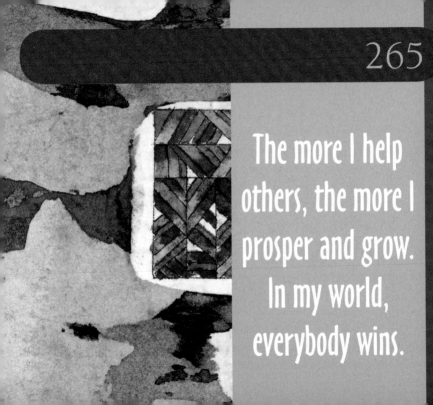

The more I help others, the more I prosper and grow. In my world, everybody wins.

Life brings
me only
positive
experiences.

The past has no power over me. I know that it is over, and I live solely in the present.

I am safe
where I am.
I create my
own security.

I give thanks
for everything
that is lovingly
supplied to me.

I see my patterns and make changes without embarrassment or guilt.

I allow my love
to flow freely.
My supply of
love is endless.

I forgive myself and set myself free.

My life is
joyously balanced
with work and
play.

I now know that I chose
my mother and father
because they were perfect
for what I had to experience
and understand.

All is well,
and even
better things
are coming.

I am very
well organized.
Life is simple
and easy.

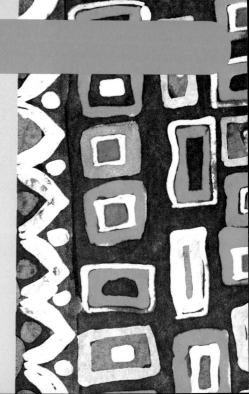

I move beyond
old limitations
and now express
myself freely
and creatively.

My unique talents
and abilities flow
through me and are
expressed in deeply
satisfying ways.

I constantly find new ways of looking at my world. I see beauty everywhere.

I choose to feel good about myself today and every day.

My life is a party to be experienced and shared with everyone I know.

282

I am willing to release
the need to be unworthy.
I am now becoming all
that I am destined to be.

I am joyously
exuberant and
in harmony with
all of life.

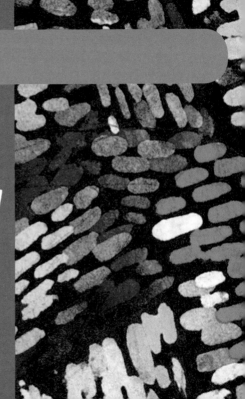

284

The people in
my life are really
mirrors of me.
My world is safe
and friendly.

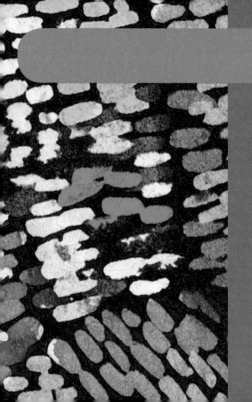

285

I handle all
my experiences
with wisdom,
love, and ease.

I think positive thoughts, because every cell within my body responds to every thought I think and every word I speak.

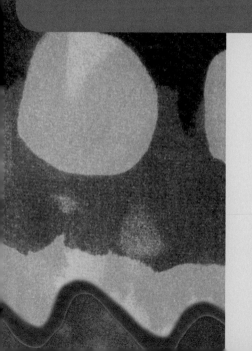

I expand my
boundaries
to encompass
only positive
experiences.

Divine peace
and harmony
surround me
at all times.

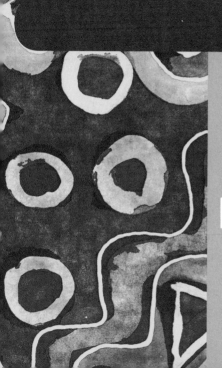

I deserve to enjoy life. I ask for what I want, and I accept it with joy and pleasure.

Working with others is part of the purpose of life.

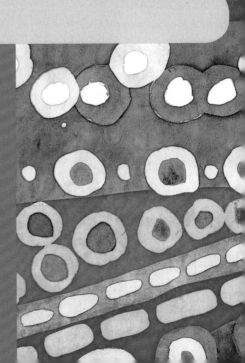

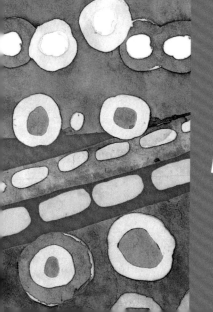

I feel good about everyone I meet. All my relationships are healthy and nourishing.

292

I am worth loving. There is love all around me.

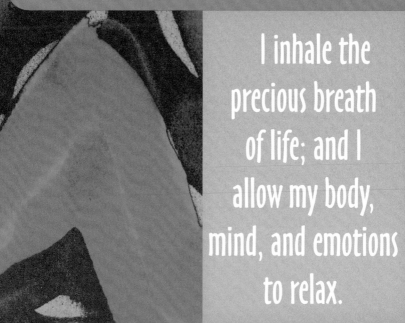

I inhale the
precious breath
of life; and I
allow my body,
mind, and emotions
to relax.

294

I take time today
to bask in the
love and light
of my life. What
a glorious day!

I take the things
I think are "wrong"
about me and turn
them into positive
affirmations.

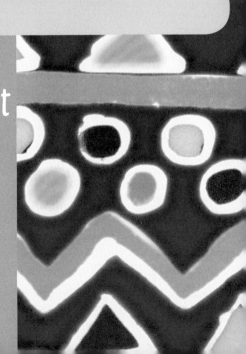

It is my birthright to share in the abundance and prosperity of this world.

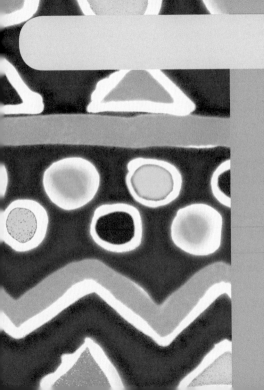

I only desire
that which
is for my
highest good.

I create miracles in my wonderful world. I am open to the wonders of the Universe.

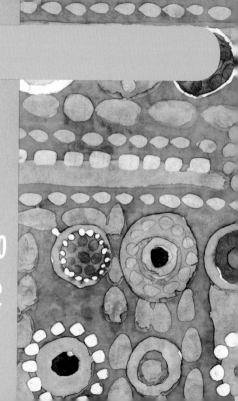

I relax,
and I recognize
my self-worth.

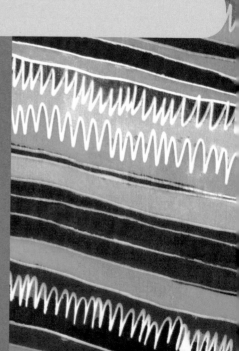

Life supports me. It brings me only good and positive experiences.

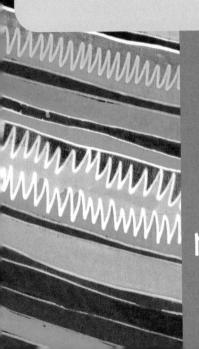

I put love in
every corner of my
home, and it lovingly
responds with warmth
and comfort.

302

I appreciate all that I do. I am the most important person in my life.

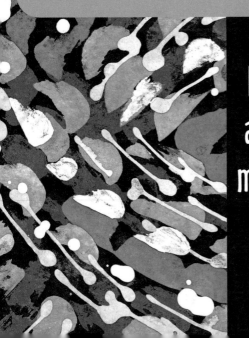

I forgive others,
and I now create
my life in the way
I wish it to be.

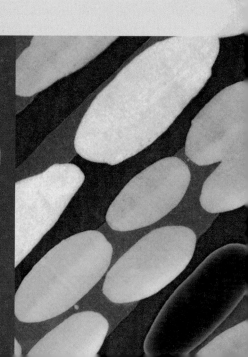

304

I make a point of setting aside a day where I just have fun!

The joy in my life is overflowing. My life gets better all the time.

Every moment
presents a wonderful
new opportunity to
become more of
who I am.

Every problem
has a solution.
Learning is easy
and fun for me.

308

I take care of my body. Water is my favorite beverage.

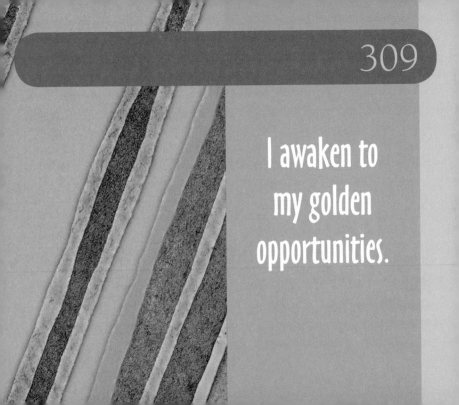

309

I awaken to
my golden
opportunities.

310

I express my
creativity openly
and freely.

I respect others
for being different,
but not wrong.
We are all one.

I see abundance radiating all around me. I now live in limitless love, light, and joy.

I have perfect faith
in the Universe
and its ability
to support my
every need.

I am willing to see how and where I need to change.

As a veteran of life,
I've learned that
guilt is useless.

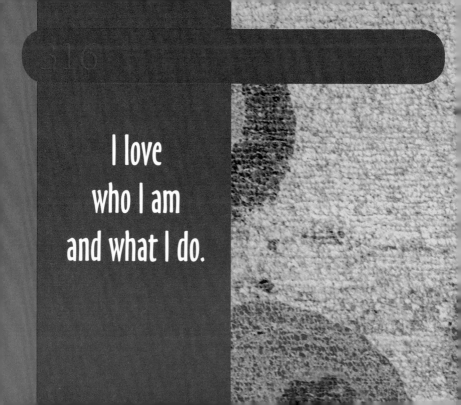

I love
who I am
and what I do.

I open my consciousness to all the wonderful possibilities of life.

Divine Intelligence gives me wonderful ideas that I apply to many different areas of my life.

I release all control
to the Universe.
I am at peace
with myself.

The pathway to
love is forgiveness.
I lovingly release the past
and turn my attention
to this new day.

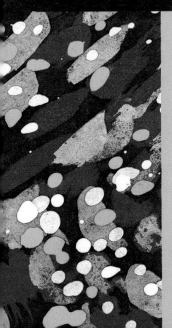

I always have wonderful, harmonious relationships. The person I am looking for is now looking for me.

I trust myself,
and I trust Life
to support and
protect me.

I treasure the loving pets in my life and treat them like family members.

324

I earn an excellent income doing what satisfies me. I know I can be as successful as I make up my mind to be.

I use my
Inner Wisdom to
run the business
of my life.

I love life.
I am glad
to be alive!

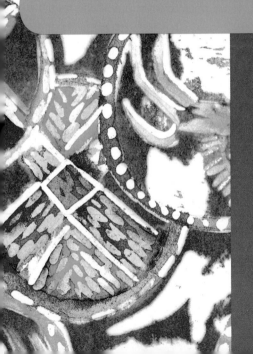

I appreciate
everyone and
everything.

I enjoy the foods that are best for me. I love every cell of my body.

I have a special
guardian angel.
I am Divinely
guided and protected
at all times.

I have the ideal neighbors. They are warmhearted and supportive.

I am quite capable
of learning new
ideas and grasping
new concepts.

I am willing to ask for help when I need it.

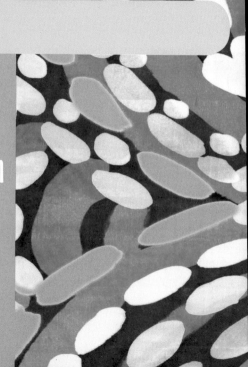

I mentally wrap
each person I meet
in a circle of love.

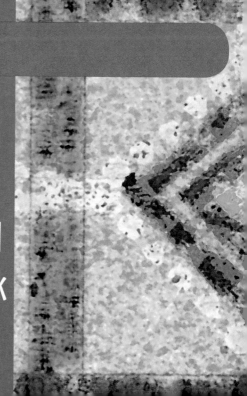

334

I now move into a new era of prosperity and abundance. Thank you, Life!

Life supports
me every step
of the way.

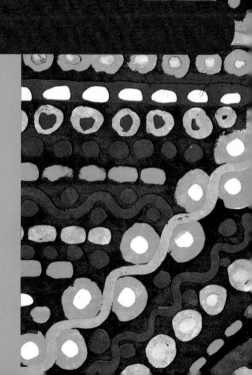

I speak up for myself. I claim my power now.

I see love in every flower, in the sun and the moon, and in every person I meet.

Every hand that touches my body is a healing hand, and I am safe.

I am grateful to
others for the
kindness they show me.
I am filled with praise
and gratitude.

I think big,
and then I allow
myself to accept
even more.

The quickest road to health is to fill my mind only with pleasant thoughts.

342

When complimented, I smile and say "Thank you." And I do not say another word to diminish it.

It is only change,
and I am safe.

I value myself by choosing nutritious foods to eat and healthy beverages to drink. I nap when my body needs a rest.

The Universe totally supports every thought I choose to think and believe.

I release the pattern of procrastination within me. I act with speed and resolve.

I am led to
fulfilling experiences.
I create a life filled
with rewards.

348

I bless my parents with love and give them the freedom to be themselves.

I carry a special feeling of joyousness with me everywhere and at all times.

I bless
this day
with love.

When I really love myself, everything in my life works.

352

I allow the love from my heart to wash through me and cleanse and heal every part of my body and emotions.

I allow change
to occur without
resistance or fear.
I am free.

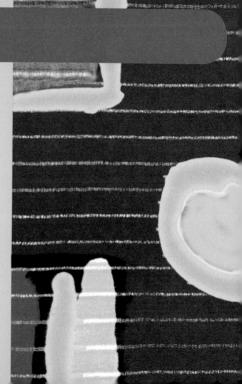

Everything that surrounds me serves a purpose.

355

Every morning
I remind myself
that I can make
the choice to
feel good.

I am willing to let go of old beliefs that no longer serve me.

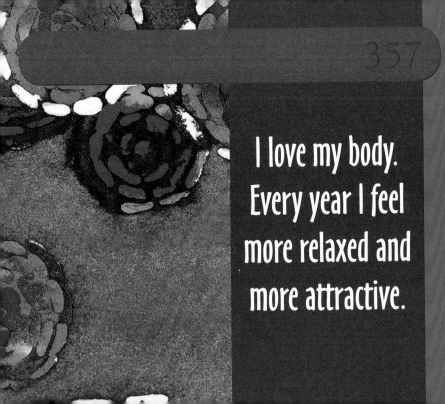

357

I love my body. Every year I feel more relaxed and more attractive.

I go back to the basics of life: forgiveness, courage, gratitude, love, and humor.

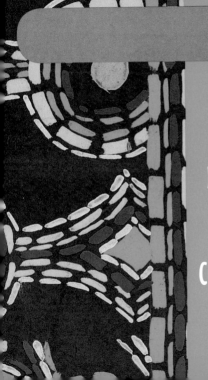

I create new memories filled with peace, goodwill, and compassion for others.

Unconditional love and acceptance are the greatest gifts I can give and receive.

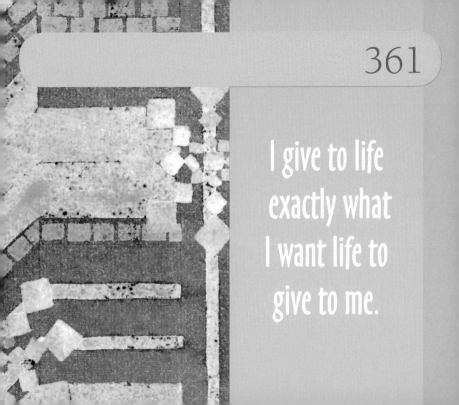

I give to life
exactly what
I want life to
give to me.

I free myself
and everyone in
my life from the
pain of the past.

I am not responsible
for other people.
We are all under
the law of our
own consciousness.

364

Something wonderful
is always coming.
I look for the good in
every experience, and
I always find it.

365

I am pleased
with what I have
created in my life.
Tomorrow is another
new beginning.

About the Author

Charles Bush

Louise Hay is a metaphysical lecturer and teacher and the best-selling author of numerous books, including *You Can Heal Your Life* and *I Can Do It®*. Her works have been translated into 29 different languages in 35 countries throughout the world. For more than 25 years, Louise has assisted millions of people in discovering and using the full potential of their own creative powers for personal growth and self-healing. Louise is the founder and chairman of Hay House, Inc., which disseminates books, audios, and videos that contribute to the healing of the planet. Website: **www.LouiseHay.com®**

***

YOU CAN HEAL YOUR LIFE, the movie,
starring Louise Hay & Friends
(available as a 1-DVD program and an expanded 2-DVD set)
Watch the trailer at: **www.LouiseHayMovie.com**

Hay House Titles of Related Interest

Everyday Wisdom for Success,
by Dr. Wayne W. Dyer

Healing Words from the Angels,
by Doreen Virtue, Ph.D.

Never Mind Success . . . Go for Greatness!
by Tavis Smiley

101 Ways to Jump-Start Your Intuition,
by John Holland

Vitamins for the Soul, by Sonia Choquette

* * *

All of the above are available at your local bookstore,
or may be ordered by visiting:

Hay House USA: **www.hayhouse.com**®
Hay House Australia: **www.hayhouse.com.au**
Hay House UK: **www.hayhouse.co.uk**
Hay House South Africa: **www.hayhouse.co.za**
Hay House India: **www.hayhouse.co.in**

Notes

Notes

Notes

Notes

Published and distributed in the United Kingdom by: Hay House UK, Ltd.,
Astley House, 33 Notting Hill Gate, London W11 3JQ • ***Phone:*** 44-20-3675-2450
Fax: 44-20-3675-2451 • www.hayhouse.co.uk

Published and distributed in the Republic of South Africa by:
Hay House SA (Pty), Ltd., P.O. Box 990, Witkoppen 2068
Phone/Fax: 27-11-467-8904 • www.hayhouse.co.za

Published in India by: Hay House Hay House Publishers India,
Muskaan Complex, Plot No. 3, B-2, Vasant Kunj, New Delhi 110 070
Phone: 91-11-4176-1620 • ***Fax:*** 91-11-4176-1630 • www.hayhouse.co.in

Distributed in Canada by: Raincoast Books, 2440 Viking Way, Richmond, B.C. V6V
1N2 • ***Phone:*** 1-800-663-5714 • ***Fax:*** 1-800-565-3770 • www.raincoast.com

❀ ❀ ❀